salisbury **in detail**

First published in Great Britain in 2009 by

Salisbury Civic Society

Registered Charity Number 293143

Congreve House
Eaglefield
Salisbury SP2 9JN

www.salisburycivicsociety.org.uk

© Salisbury Civic Society 2009

ISBN 978-0-9512100-1-7

Printed by Information Press Ltd,
Southfield Road, Eynsham, Oxford, OX29 4JB

salisbury **in detail**

Salisbury Civic Society

contributors

Concept and text   Richard Deane

Graphic design and production © 2009   Louise Rendell
Melanie Latham
James Salman

Photography   Alastair Clark
Richard Deane
Melanie Latham
Simon Lock
Louise Rendell
Paul Stevens
John Sykes
Charles Villiers

With thanks to John Elliott for his publishing advice and guidance and all those consulted through various stages of the book's development and production.

contents

Dedicated to Jim & Margaret Drew

who loved the city and without whom

this book would not have been possible.

I built in the grounds of my house a building of oak and stone and good old-fashioned lime mortar. Inside, the light changes subtly throughout the day; lime plaster and distemper make buildings live.

When it was finished I found a young stonemason to carve a little tableau into one of the gables. In the best tradition of these sorts of things, it can only be found by them as knows where to look, and it shows me handing bags of gold to the foreman of the builders and to the architect. I like to think that in 100 years' time people will look at it and say "what the hell is that all about?" but I feel happy about it being there, because the stonemason was Jason Battle, of this parish, and the next time I saw him he was putting the new cross on Salisbury Cathedral. Details are important.

We don't seem to put them in our buildings now; we have design. We don't raise weathervanes in cold blood, because most of us live lives in which the wind's direction and force have no relevance. There is no room overhead for domes and cupolas. The flat roofs of most buildings these days tend to resemble a junk yard. We seldom need boot scrapers because for most of us there is seldom mud underfoot; but a chewing gum scraper might be a worthwhile modern invention. I regret, though, that it might not be allowed to have its own iron gargoyle...

These simple things, often battered, sometimes unseen until pointed out, sometimes an architect's delight, sometimes a builder's happy flourish, are presents from the past, reminding us that things were not always thus, and that any man desiring to drive his pony and trap into his house could simply bash a bigger hole in his own wall without one clipboard being raised in anger. They tell us that real people really did real things here, and in a quiet way still are doing them. Architectural details are important. They may be made of brick and stone and wood, but in the end they are resolutely human.

Terry Pratchett

Few cities are dominated by a single building in quite the way that Salisbury is by its cathedral. Few announce themselves, even when everything else remains hidden, with a single skywards marker, the upper spire that fixes the destination for those coming down the main road from Amesbury, or over the downs from Odstock. And very few owe their entire existence to a cathedral, to a building set down on a meadow bordered by no more than a couple of sparse hamlets, and then summoning up a city around itself.

So perhaps it is slightly perverse that this is a book about the buildings of Salisbury which will, from here on, contain no further acknowledgement of the cathedral other than a single distorted reflection of its west front. The book, in fact, takes two steps back from that astonishing structure at the city's heart, and indeed from all its churches. It is about the rich and varied array of other buildings that go to make up the whole city, but even here there is barely a single image of a complete building.

The book is indeed about Salisbury's 'detail', about the individual elements that fit together to form those buildings, that develop overall designs to shape the streets first laid out almost 800 years ago. So it is a book about doors and windows and chimneys and brick patterns and gables, and only indirectly about the houses and shops and schools created out of those individual parts. And in bypassing the broad picture in favour of the detail behind it, the book reveals a truth about the city which it is all too easy to overlook. Salisbury's character as a historic city would generally be considered to be a creation of historic architecture, of structures whose age and design aspirations mark them out as notable and worthy of protection, and specifically of being 'listed', which means they cannot be altered without the planners' consent.

A book such as this, which celebrates that architecture, might therefore be expected to deal mostly with listed buildings. And indeed there are many in these pages, contributing their carefully designed doorcases and windows, their carvings in stone and wood, their turrets and cupolas and finials. But there is another story being told here as well, because out of more than 500 images in the book, almost half come from buildings which are not listed. For the most part, these structures do not fall within the city's fairly tightly defined conservation area either - in other words, they have no form of statutory protection at all. They are fringe buildings, both geographically and in terms of official attitudes towards them, but they are in this book because they contain some element beyond the utilitarian and mundane, something that is worth stopping to look at.

What we are talking about here, mainly, are the Victorian and Edwardian suburbs, the 19th and early 20th century expansion that took the city eastwards into Milford, westwards into Lower Bemerton, southwards into Harnham. Mostly speculative development, generating pleasant housing that generally fails to catch the attention of the listing authorities, but whose creators still felt it was worth making the effort to do a bit more than just put up walls with some openings in them and a roof on top. Moulded terracotta, elaborate chimneys, doorways carefully framed and topped with decorative timber or leadwork, quirky bootscrapers - all contributing to a subtle extra layer of visual value, enhancing these parts of the city as places for living in or passing through, even if the eye seldom focuses on the individual elements for very long.

There is a final part to the story as well, conspicuous in this book only by its absence. Very little here dates from much after 1920. A visually bleaker early modern world seems to have emerged around then, where, in domestic architecture at least, ornament was either half-hearted or missing completely. This does not mean that good design as a whole died out, of course, but the aspect of it covered by this book certainly suffered. By the latter years of the 20th century the instinct to add decoration, or to design standard building components to add value to the whole, had been replaced in housing developments by what amounted to little more than gesture-making. Half-hearted replicas of traditional details, added when the context (or the planners) required it, and failing almost every time when compared with the genuine detail across the road. The 21st century contributes just three photographs to this book, none of them from a house.

All the more important, then, to value what we have, since the source for it has dried up. The listed buildings in this book are generally safe from harm (to their exteriors, at least). The unlisted ones are pretty well on their own, even the ones in conservation areas, which are given only very sparse protection. The chief resource for looking after such buildings is simply awareness - appreciation of what makes them special, and unwillingness to let irreplaceable details go simply because timber has to be painted and plastic doesn't, or a chimney is no longer functionally essential.

This book, besides its chief purpose of celebrating the richness and variety of the individual bits that go to make up Salisbury's buildings, has therefore an added aim of making clear how much of its visual appeal lies beyond the obvious candidates in the historic core. Salisbury may be a medieval city, as the car park signs tell us, but it is much more than that. From the book's perspective, Manor Road and Fowlers Hill and corners beyond are as important as the Close - there are good bits in unexpected places, and the book will have succeeded if it presents some picture of what there is to be valued across all the city's buildings, however grand or humble.

01

doorways

The external doorway as essential functional element obviously came first, but the doorway as a design opportunity probably followed not far behind. Front doors in particular have always been a prime focus of the instinct to treat a building as more than just a box with holes in it, and the ways in which this opportunity can be exploited are almost limitless. The following pages show a few of them, ranging from the simple to the grand, and from the stylistically orthodox to the completely unfathomable. The pair on this page are unusual, since the doorways are 50 or more years earlier than the houses in which they sit. They almost certainly did not start life as door surrounds, but have been formed out of elements from some other type of decoration, possibly framing for large paintings. Such paintings were often mounted on the walls of grand Georgian rooms, but if the house changed hands they would probably move on with the owner, and a moulded surround might be recycled elsewhere. The slightly heavy style of these pieces, which is likely to date them to the first half of the 18th century, is rather at odds with that of the houses in Exeter Street into which they were incorporated, which can be dated to around 1800. The overall effect, however, does not jar at all.

01

this page:
1. North Walk, The Close
2. & 3. Crane Street
4. Catherine Street
5. Love Lane
6. Harcourt Terrace

facing page:
1. North Walk, The Close
2. Brewery Lane
3. West Walk, The Close
4. Bedwin Street
5. Choristers' Green, The Close
6. Bedwin Street
7. North Walk, The Close
8. St Edmund's Church Street

salisbury **in detail**

Second from the right at the top of this page is a doorway from Frowds Almshouses, in Bedwin Street, relatively unusual because it bears the marks of the sometimes rather ponderous baroque style, popular in the early part of the 18th century. The almshouses' date of 1750 indicates that the door is a late example of the style. Rather more typical of Salisbury's buildings is the doorway at bottom centre on this page from the Close, with its lighter late 18th century classical design. The other Bedwin Street doorway, bottom left, is from Taylors Almshouses, and reverts to an earlier style, but in fact dates from a rebuilding in 1886, and how much

it was influenced by the main doorway of the previous 1698 building is unclear. What is visible now is actually later than either of those dates, since all the Ham Hill stonework was renewed in 2002. The St Edmund's Church Street doorway, bottom right on this page, dates from 1787, as can be seen on a rainwater head which appears on page 67. The house was formerly the premises of Messrs Rouse, sellers of ropes and tarpaulins, and in the 1970s and 80s the office inside recalled another period again, decorated as it was with 1950s calendars and other rather faded leftovers from that distant age.

The doorway on the facing page is without doubt the most remarkable in the whole city. It contains a standard size door, but the real story is told by the hinges visible to the right, within two of the alternating long and short blocks, or quoins. When these hinges still functioned the whole bottom corner of the building was able to move, door surround and all. The house was apparently at one time occupied by a doctor, who kept a horse and trap in stables behind the doorway. When word came of a medical emergency, his servants would fling open the corner of the house, and the doctor would charge out on his mission of mercy. In the later years of the 20th century integral garages were quite often features of suburban houses, but they never came close to matching the elegance of this 18th century equivalent.

this page:
1. St Ann Street
2. North Walk, The Close

facing page:
St Ann Street

this page:
1. Rollestone Street
2. Bourne Hill

facing page:
1 & 2. Choristers' Green, The Close

The front door and stable doors on this page date from the middle part of the 18th century, though the lacy fanlight in the former looks like a change or addition of about 50 years later. Both are part of the service ranges to Mompesson House. On the facing page the doorway in the boundary wall to the Council House in Bourne Hill probably dates from the mid-18th century refacing of the whole house, while the Rollestone Street example is rather different in style. It is part of a garden wall, early 17th century in date, to a house in Endless Street. The shape of its arch is typical of a late medieval tradition which lingered on well into the post-medieval period, and can be seen in many fireplaces of the 16th and 17th centuries. The lower parts of the wall to either side are original, but the upper parts may well be 20th century.

this page:
1. Castle Street
2. West Walk, The Close

facing page:
Wilton Road

Two of the three doorways on these pages have a rather sad look about them, and it is not a surprise that they are the ones made from wood, unlike the example in Chilmark stone of around 1720 from the Walton Canonry, in the Close. Timber doors and their surrounds, particularly softwood ones, need to be protected by regular repainting, and if they have lead coverings, as the late 18th century Castle Street one does, these will not last for ever. Prolonged neglect is likely to lead to major expense when repairs are eventually made, and in the worst cases it may no longer be clear precisely what the original design looked like.

this page:
1. St Ann Street
2. Crane Street
3. Castle Street
4. Choristers' Green, The Close
5. School Lane
6. Choristers' Green, The Close

facing page:
Crane Bridge Road

facing page:
1. St Ann Street
2. Paynes Hill
3. Bedwin Street
4. New Street

this page:
1. West Walk, The Close
2. Endless Street
3. St Edmund's Church Street
4. St Ann Street
5. North Walk, The Close

The double doorway on this page, from London Road, belongs to a pair of semi-detached houses, probably dating from around 1880. They are remarkable for the ornateness and quality of their carved Gothic decoration, in Bath stone, which is not paralleled anywhere else in Salisbury's domestic architecture, and not that often in its churches. The explanation appears to be that the houses were constructed for themselves by a pair of brothers who were builders, and possibly even stonemasons. They were therefore able to add a level of detail which would never be found in purely speculative housing.

this page:
1. London Road
2. The Greencroft

facing page:
Harcourt Terrace

2

3

4

The two Castle Street doorways on this page illustrate how, in Salisbury, stylistic variations from the Georgian norm generally affected bits of buildings, not whole ones. Of these two the style of the left-hand one cannot be pinned down much more than the description 'exotic', while the one on the right has the fretwork patterning known as 'Chinese Chippendale', typical of its date of around 1760. The house behind is actually 15th century. On the facing page the St Nicholas Road red doorway is probably medieval, while the date and inspiration of the Castle Street one are a mystery. The most apt description is probably 'weird'.

this page:
1. Castle Street
2. College Street

3. Railway Station
4. Castle Street

facing page:
1. Barnard Street
2. St Nicholas Road
3. Castle Street
4. St Nicholas Road

5. Wain-a-long Road
6. Behind Crane Street
7. Wyndham Road

salisbury **in detail**

this page:
1. North Walk, The Close
2. Harcourt Terrace

facing page:
North Walk, The Close

02

bootscrapers

Traditional urban house designs of the 18th and 19th centuries tend to be so successful visually that they are often copied today, with results of varying levels of success. One element that invariably gets lost along the way is the bootscraper, a once essential feature whose function in towns has simply disappeared. The age of horse transport may seem very attractive from the perspective of today's traffic-polluted streets, but the inevitable equine fall-out that went with it was rather less romantic. Anywhere on a route to Salisbury market place, when that still functioned as a livestock market, would have been treated to an even greater number of random organic deposits. The bootscraper is a silent reminder of a very different sort of street. Stylistically they tend to go their own way, seldom picking up on the major architectural themes of the day, and precise dating is difficult, though it may be safe to ascribe most of the recessed examples to the 19th century. What is clear is that they tended to be a standard item in cast iron, with most of the scrapers in the city centre belonging to one of only three basic patterns. The one from New Street on this page is in fact virtually identical to the scraper from St Edmund's Church Street two pages on, apart from having a different face at the top of it.

02

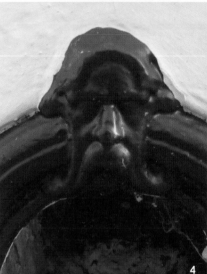

this page:
1. Bedwin Street
2. Milford Hill
3. School Lane
4. New Street

facing page:
St Edmund's Church Street

The Bedwin Street scraper is recessed, which is the usual form for houses fronting onto the pavement. In less constricted areas, away from the town centre, freestanding types are more common. Out of all five on these pages, only the Bedwin Street example has any real relationship to mainstream design styles, with its anthemion at the top of the curved opening. This is a classical Greek motif, based on the honeysuckle flower, but the rest of the scraper is less orthodox. The one from New Street again has a face in the focal position, though here the remaining parts are not a duplicate of others in the city.

salisbury **in detail**

On this page the square scraper maintains a sturdy tradition of independence from identifiable design sources, with its vertical lines going nowhere, but the green one is slightly more orthodox. The 'ogee', or double-curved, shape was often used around 1350, and appeared again when the Gothic style was revived in the late 18th century. Once the revival had become serious, by about 1830, the shape was deemed to be too frivolous and decadent, and this may date the scraper to the early years of the 19th century. This sort of analysis would certainly be applicable to a major building feature, but whether it really works for bootscrapers is another matter. On the facing page, the Castle Street scraper is at the foot of the doorcase shown on page 18, and shares its rather shabby appearance. Whereas failing paintwork on the doorcase is a major cause for concern, however, the bootscraper is made of sterner stuff, and its cast ironwork, which is no doubt Victorian in date, will succumb to rust far more slowly than a softwood will perish under the insidious advance of wet rot.

this page:
1. Castle Street
2. New Street
3. Off Choristers' Green, The Close
4. North Walk, The Close

facing page:
1 & 2. Off Choristers' Green, The Close

03

door furniture

To come under the heading of door furniture, an object needs to be permanently fixed to a door, or its frame, and to have some function. In practice, it is likely to be made of metal, and its function may well just be a base for the addition of ornamentation. Few stray outside a list comprising handles, letter boxes, door knockers and bell pushes, plus the occasional inscribed brass plate. Unusually for the features covered in this book, such items often have no connection with their building as originally constructed, and they are generally very hard to date. But this hardly matters, and to worry about when the pieces in the following pages were made would be to miss the point. Door knockers in particular give house owners a unique opportunity to add their own highly visible stamp to a property, and the outcome is a wide range of objects, from the commonplace to the beautiful or the eccentric. Occasionally they are fixed in time, like the celebration of Winston Churchill which records the dates of his birth and death, but generally they occupy a timeless world, unconcerned with styles of the day, converting the tastes of a house's occupants into visible displays which can lift the spirits as we pass by, if we just pause and notice them.

03

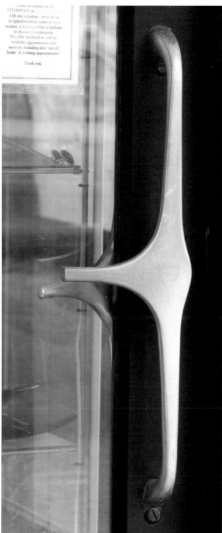
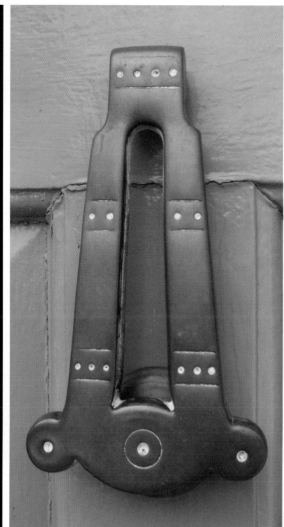

salisbury **in detail**

door furniture

04

brickwork

Medieval Salisbury was principally a town of timber-frame, and to a lesser extent stone, with brick buildings probably more or less unknown before 1600. When they did arrive, they would invariably be of red brick, until the second half of the 18th century when national tastes changed, and buff-coloured bricks became fashionable. The demand for these was met locally by brickworks in the Devizes Road area, exploiting a seam of clay there to produce Fisherton Grey bricks. The main works were on a site later occupied by a Nestlé factory, and now by housing. Red bricks were not made in the city, with the most important local source being at Whaddon, on the edge of Alderbury. After the middle of the 19th century multi-coloured or 'polychromatic' brickwork came into fashion, best seen in Salisbury here at the former Art College in New Street. This makes use of local red and white/grey bricks, mixed with ones of dull blue colour, quite possibly local, and garishly blue ones. These highly glazed products were certainly not local, most probably coming from Cannock, in the Midlands.

04

1. St Martin's Church Street
2. Milford Street

Two windows of the early 19th century, one using local red bricks and the other Fisherton Greys. In both cases the tops of the windows, which are technically arches even though they are more or less flat, have been formed in gauged brickwork. This term covers work where bricks have been precisely shaped and put together using very tight joints, ideally no more than 2mm in width, though this can be masked by later repointing. To achieve this level of precision, special bricks known as 'rubbers' were made, using finer and purer clay than the usual material. These were then sawn and sanded into the required shape, by hand.

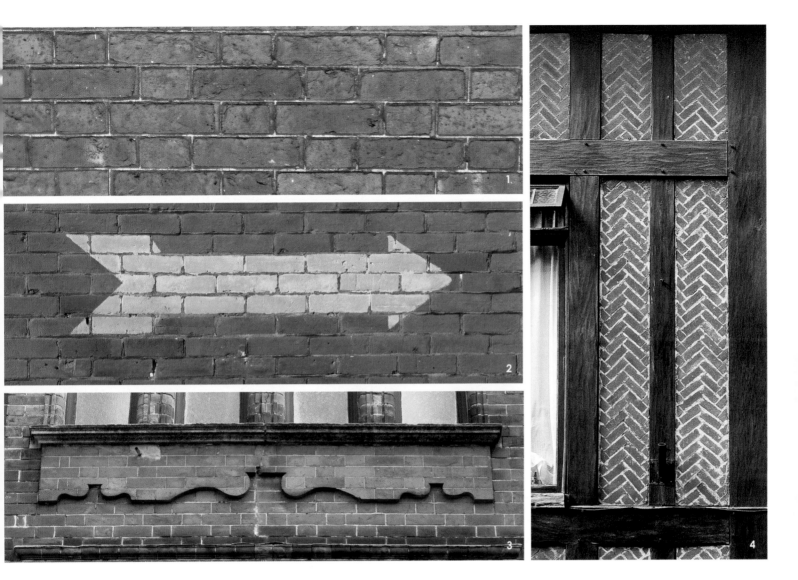

The Georgian brickwork from Brown Street shows techniques used at the time to give a more consistent overall appearance. A reddish wash has been applied, using ingredients such as venetian red (a pigment) and ox blood, with results now best seen on the joints. These have also been 'penny pointed', by scoring with a metal disc. The resulting narrow grooves were in this case then filled with lime pointing, now mostly gone. The arrow in the photograph below points the way to the now vanished Nestlé factory, off the Devizes Road, or perhaps to the brickworks which preceded it. To the right the herringbone pattern is one quite often used to infill panels in timber-framed buildings of the 17th century onwards, though this is in fact an example from the 20th century. At the bottom of the page, the shaped feature below a window is known as an apron, and is another example of gauged brickwork, with the shape cut in situ after the bricks were positioned.

1. Brown Street
2. Russell Road
3. Minster Street
4. Catherine Street

this page:
1 & 2. Catherine Street
3. Wyndham Road

facing page:
Manor Road

On this page there are two examples of diamond-shaped, or 'diaper' patterns, achieved in the case of Catherine Street by using bricks with a bluish glazed finish, a result of their being fired near the centre of the kiln, where temperatures were highest. In the gable of 1882 from the same street, ornamental brickwork has been formed by using 'specials', bricks moulded to particular shapes. The facing page shows a gable from a house in Manor Road called Hillcote, where a triangular panel has been built up in gauged brickwork and then carved in situ, using techniques essentially the same as those of stonecarving.

salisbury **in detail**

While many of the architectural details in this book are types which offer several examples to choose from, some were seldom if ever repeated elsewhere. The decoration shown above, from a short terrace in Tollgate Road of around 1900, was quite possibly used in no other building, locally or anywhere else. Thin pieces of flint have been cut into squares and set in mortar, to create a mosaic around the tops of doors and windows. This has all been done by hand, involving a major amount of work even by the standards of the time. A speculative housing development today would struggle to achieve anything remotely similar. When new

houses next door were being planned in 2006, similar decoration was suggested for them, but the idea never got very far. This is probably just as well, given that most modern attempts to replicate traditional detailing from houses tend to fall alarmingly short of the originals.

this page: Tollgate Road
facing page: 1. St Ann Street
               2. Guilder Lane
               3. West Walk, The Close

05

gables & eaves

Two parts of a building that make the functionally essential junction between walls and roof, but also offer opportunities for decoration. This can range from orthodox elements based on classical precedents, to opportunist one-offs in the realm of the unusual or the frankly bizarre. The example on this page, from a house opposite the west front of the cathedral, combines both approaches. In its overall format the design is typically Georgian, until the point where the continuous moulding below the gutter is supplemented by a row of motifs of no identifiable antecedent. The ornament is hard to describe or relate to any conventional

artefact, although a very tentative suggestion might be made that it vaguely resembles an upside-down wooden toy soldier. However the idea came into the designer's mind, the overall effect is all the more valuable for not coming from a standard pattern book.

05

1. Minster Street
2. Wilton Road
3. Belle Vue Road

The Minster Street gable at the top left uses fairly orthodox motifs in its sides, but the vertical feature at the apex is less conventional. Its incised decoration includes, half-way up, what looks remarkably like the Chinese character for 'big', but this is hardly likely to be deliberate. Equally individual, but perhaps with hindsight slightly melancholy, is the Belle Vue Road gable, whose date of 1914 ties it to what can now be seen as the end of an era. One world war and a catastrophic flu epidemic later, housebuilding seems to have entered a different world where this kind of unselfconscious elegance was beyond its aspirations.

1. Silver Street
2. School Lane
3. West Walk, The Close
4. Bishop's Walk, The Close
5. Milford Street
6. North Walk, The Close
7. New Canal

All the gables on these two pages and the next two have wooden bargeboards, which hide the structural timbers on each roof slope. Their potential for decoration was frequently exploited in medieval and post-medieval Salisbury, to such an extent that 18th and 19th century visitors often mentioned them when writing about the city. The 14th century pair from New Canal, bottom right on the previous page, are the only bargeboards to actually survive from the Middle Ages, but there are many replacements of medieval originals, and others from later periods, all adding to the visual richness of the city's buildings.

this page:
Southampton Road

facing page:
1. New Street
2. Belle Vue Road
3. Crane Street
4. West Walk, The Close

5. Estcourt Road
6. Castle Street
7. Lower Road
8. Wilton Road

salisbury **in detail**

this page:
1. Minster Street
2 & 3. Queen Street

facing page:
1. Minster Street
2. St Ann Street
3. New Canal

There is further evidence on these pages that gables and bargeboards lent themselves to a wealth of decorative detail, often based on the Gothic style. The Odeon gable, on the right of the facing page, merits particular scrutiny. Nineteenth century in date, its quality is a worthy match for that of the 15th century hall which forms the cinema's inner foyer, and typical of its designer, a Salisbury architect called Fred Bath, whose name will reappear in later sections. The bear that stands proudly on the apex has gazed out over the city since 1881, probably noticed by only a small fraction of the people passing below.

salisbury **in detail**

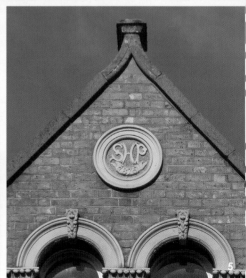

salisbury **in detail**

The date of 1895 on the Fisherton Street gable, top left on the facing page, is probably not far off the mark for all the gables on these two pages. Both the one from Fisherton Street and the one below it, from Manor Road, have window patterns typical of the years around 1900, with the upper sash divided by glazing bars but a single piece of glass in the lower one. What doesn't fit into a neat 'end of the 19th century' pattern is the finial at the top of the Manor Road gable, which has an art deco look to it. This is a style of the 1920s and 30s, so the finial is either a later addition, or remarkably ahead of its time.

this page:
St Mark's Road

facing page:
1. Fisherton Street
2. Bridge Street
3. Manor Road
4. Milford Manor Gardens
5. Elm Grove Road

gables & eaves

this page:
1. Ox Row
2. Fowlers Hill
3. Railway Station
4. School Lane

facing page:
Behind Bedwin Street

Salisbury railway station, bottom left on this page, is a building of considerable merit, though it had to wait till 2008 to achieve listed status. It was constructed in two phases, with this gable dating from the later one of 1902. The stone set within it, declaring a date of 1881, which isn't even that of the earlier phase, is therefore more than a little misleading. Bottom right is a gable from a former school on the western edge of St Edmund's Churchyard, about which more can be discovered on page 69.

salisbury **in detail**

06

downpipes & gutters

What importance one places on dealing with rainwater in the design of a building pretty clearly has a direct relationship with geography, and while Salisbury is not really in one of the wetter regions of the world, it would be foolish to deny that rainwater disposal has been more to the fore in the minds of builders and architects than it would have been in, say, Cairo. The results show that the old adage about making a virtue out of necessity has been invoked on a regular basis, with some nice decorative flourishes being applied to the mundane realities of getting water off a roof. The most common focus for this is the hopper head,

which gathers water from gutters and feeds it into downpipes. Initials and/or dates are often added, as in the example above from St Edmund's Church Street. The most traditional material for hopper heads and downpipes, though not for suspended gutters which came later, was lead, with cast iron making an appearance in the 19th century. In more recent times mild steel, aluminium and in particular plastic have taken over, and in the process attempts at decoration have more or less been abandoned.

06

this page:
1. Victoria Road
2. Choristers' Green, The Close

facing page:
1. Butcher Row
2. Chipper Lane
3. North Walk, The Close
4. High Street
5. School Lane

A variety of shapes appear on these pages, some in lead and some in cast iron, and with decoration both through initials and dates, and through added flourishes. The bastion-enriched iron hopper head from Victoria Road on the facing page was clearly a stock item, available from a manufacturer or through a wholesaler around 1900 - identical heads can be seen on a terrace on the south side of Exeter. On this page the example bottom right, with the date 1860, is on a former school to the west of the Arts Centre, already glimpsed on page 64. It is a type often used by its architect, Henry Woodyer, though it does not do justice to the intensity of his best work, which was driven by strong religious convictions. In Berkshire he designed a 'home for fallen women' across a period of over 40 years, without ever charging a fee. The Salisbury school is relatively restrained, but it is of interest because its interior contains a stone fireplace and timber roof which are 15th century in date. They were originally in the Maidenhead Inn, in the Cheesemarket, and were rescued and re-used here after that building was pulled down in 1858 to make way for the Market House, whose facade survives as the front of the present library.

The New Street hopper head on the facing page is a very early example of one with an added date. Used relatively thinly as a roofing material, lead may not last much more than 100 years, but the much thicker type used for downpipes has enabled this piece of plumber's work to quietly survive for over 400. The identity of the 'TR' who commissioned or made it is however probably lost forever. While many modern plumbers will never have to deal with lead at all, the name of their trade retains its early connection with the material, derived as it is from 'plumbum', the Latin word for the metal.

this page:
1. North Walk, The Close
2. Winchester Street

facing page:
New Street

07

blind windows

Blind windows were often never windows at all, but design features which were blank from the start. They might for instance be used to maintain the symmetry of a facade, where the internal layout did not require a full set of openings. Many do however result from the blocking up of former windows, very often no doubt in response to the national window tax, first imposed on houses in 1696. Its details varied over the years, but in general it was certainly an incentive towards having a reduced number of windows. The tax's abolition in 1851 will have been applauded, even if its rapid replacement by the new-fangled income tax

can only have been seen as a case of 'out of the frying pan into the fire'. Some blocked windows will be a consequence of later alterations or extensions making a window redundant, rather than of tax considerations. For the example shown above, the route to its present state was different again. It is about all that remains of The Barracks, a high status 15th century house in Brown Street, most of which was demolished in the second half of the 19th century. The blocking of this melancholy fragment no doubt dates from that period.

07

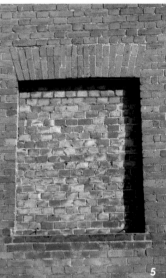

1. Milford Street
2. Rosemary Lane, The Close
3. West Walk, The Close
4. Fisherton Street
5. St Ann Street

The Milford Street blind window, on the left, is probably the result of an originally functional window being blocked, though the brickwork of the infill is not obviously different from that around it, and the blocking must have happened early in the building's life. The example bottom right, from St Ann Street, seems more likely to have been blind from the start, with the infill deliberately carried out in a different style. The bricks are all 'headers', i.e. they are laid end on, and they have been selected to be predominantly 'vitrified' ones, meaning they have been fired at high enough temperatures to form a bluish glaze on the surface.

The example on the right of this page, from the Close, was clearly once a proper opening, and it still retains within its blocking the original 17th century 'mullion and transom' form of the window, making up a cross shape (the mullion is the vertical part, and the transom the horizontal one). Most of the other windows in the house have been converted to take sashes. The blocked window from Fisherton Street is one of two surviving from the former city prison, and is only a few feet from the bridge which carries the road over the Avon. Both windows are hidden from view by trees and ivy. The stretch of wall containing them, together with a carved plaque which can be seen on page 171, survive because they were used in the base for a clocktower constructed in 1890. This is illustrated in the section on sundials and clockfaces.

1. Bourne Hill
2. Fisherton Street
3. Bishop's Walk, The Close

1. Endless Street
2. North Walk, The Close
3. Choristers' Green, The Close

The plastered-over Close window, with its projecting hoodmould, is typical in form of the 16th or 17th century, but is probably actually Victorian. The other example from the Close was also originally a functioning window, but how the blocking-up came to done behind the line of the wall, leaving the vertical bars freestanding, is unclear.

This recess, one of a pair at the Guildhall, has no doubt always been blind. The infill uses mathematical tiles, a form of cladding employed in the later 18th century and for much of the 19th to look like brickwork. It was often used when earlier buildings were being refaced in the latest style, and works so well that the many examples in Salisbury just look like brick buildings to most passers-by. The black tiles seen here are not found elsewhere in Salisbury, and probably came from Sussex, where their glazed finish was used to protect seafront buildings, for instance at Brighton. On the right of the page, the more typical red mathematical tiles from St Ann Street are exposed at one edge and unpointed on the face, and show how the illusion of brickwork is created. How the name 'mathematical' became attached to this sort of tile is not clear, though it may be intended to indicate the precision with which they needed to be made. An alternative name was 'weather tiles', a reference to the protective function which they had when used to clad older buildings.

1. The Guildhall
2 & 3. St Ann Street

08

windows

The remarkable variety of forms that windows can take is illustrated in one of the book's longest sections. The photo above, from St Ann Street, shows one design theme at its height - the classic Georgian sash window, here with shutters both external and internal, gauged brick arches, stone cills and keystones, and surrounded by tightly jointed and warmly coloured brickwork. Suffusing the whole is that subtle perfection of proportion which the Georgian style seemed to be able to achieve almost without effort. Timber sash windows continued long after the end of the period, into the early part of the 20th century, and quietly make a fundamental contribution to the quality of many buildings across those years, even quite humble ones. Or at least they used to - one of the most profound changes in the modern period, to houses in particular, has been the insertion of replacement windows, most often of plastic. Usually the pattern changes as well as the material, and the subtle three dimensional effect involved in one sash being set back behind the other is lost. The original glass, often with a character lacking in the smooth perfection of the modern material, also disappears. With one exception, the photos on these pages record windows in their original forms, crucial contributors to many of the city's most valued buildings.

08

this page:
1. St Ann Street
2. Tollgate Road
3. St Ann's Gate, The Close
4. Milford Street
5. Exeter Street
6. Gigant Street
7. St Martin's Church Street
8. Choristers' Green, The Close

facing page:
1. New Canal
2. Minster Street
3. New Street

The half-round window from New Street, on this page, recalls the style of Robert Adam, highly influential in English architecture during the three decades from around 1760. Styles tended to filter down only slowly to Salisbury, now something of a provincial backwater after its medieval eminence, and this house may date from soon after 1800. The Adam style no longer extends to the whole building, as half the ground floor is now an integral garage, still with the remains of a fireplace in it. This is alas somewhat less elegant than the integral stables in St Ann Street, referred to in the doors section of the book.

this page:
1 & 2. Chipper Lane
3. Brown Street

facing page:
Minster Street

Four examples from what was something of a Golden Age for buildings in Salisbury, the two decades centred on 1900. On the facing page is New Sarum House, a building seen more than once elsewhere in the book. On this page the Young Gallery was started in 1910, and top right is its neighbour immediately to the east, originally built as Salisbury's first public library, and dated 1905. Its architect was Alfred Champney Bothams, who could keep an eye on construction without stirring from his office, since this was directly opposite at No 32 Chipper Lane. The art nouveau glass from Brown Street also dates from this period around 1900.

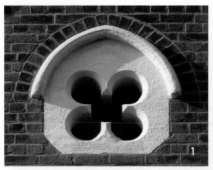

this page:
1. Milford Street
2. Rollestone Street
3. Ox Row
4. Castle Road

facing page:
1. Manor Road
2. Salt Lane
3. St Ann's Gate, The Close

The house from Castle Road was built in or just before 1930. It is a fairly late example of the Arts and Crafts style, which shows itself here in the uneven white render, the use of tiles for the arch to the door, and the angled buttress to its left. The window is cleverly contrived as an insertion into the roof slope. The house was designed by the Salisbury architects' practice which was also responsible for the former public library, on the previous page. At the time the Castle Road house was built, the practice was called Bothams and Brown, and with slight variations of name it worked from the same offices from 1883 up until the late 1990s.

salisbury **in detail**

The Manor Road window is from Hillcote, a house that appears in several other sections of the book. This is a tribute to the verve and inventiveness of its architect, Fred Bath, who practised from Crown Chambers, on the north side of Bridge Street. During the latter part of the 19th century, and the early years of the 20th, he produced a steady output of high quality buildings, several of them alas since demolished, including the Chinese-styled Victoria Park pavilion. Hillcote, dated 1896, is a particularly fine example of his work. This window, with its classically derived terracotta ornamentation, provides additional light for the drawing room,

just to the right of which is a space originally used as an aviary. This feature, unusual for any period, was presumably requested by the man of means for whom the house was built, whose identity for once we know. He was called Ambrose Tucker, and his initials, on the side of the house, can be seen on page 167. The Salt Lane window has a profusion of pointed arch shapes, and is a good example of the style known as gothick. The additional 'k' denotes the rather playful late 18th century interpretation of the medieval style, more serious versions of which are known as Gothic.

Three pieces of domestic stained glass, the Dews Road and Manor Road ones both known to be from the 1890s, and the Rectory Road one, on the right of the facing page, probably similar in date. It is a particularly fine example, from a porch with two other windows of equal quality, an internal feature which can still be appreciated by passers-by whenever the porch door is open. The techniques used to create this glass reflect the Victorian revival of the medieval stained glass tradition, together with one or two post-medieval additions to the craft, such as enamelling. The coloured glass is created by various techniques.

One type, known as 'pot metal', has the colour right through, but the red will almost certainly be thin red glass bonded to clear, to prevent the colour being too deep. This is known as 'flashed glass'. Yellow is the only type obtained by true 'staining', whereby silver nitrate is painted on, and then absorbed into the glass by firing in a kiln. The pieces of glass are joined together by grooved sections of lead, into which they are secured by a compound similar to putty. The basic techniques of stained glass have hardly changed since the Middle Ages.

salisbury **in detail**

this page:
1. Manor Road
2. Rectory Road

facing page:
Dews Road

this page:
1. Fisherton Street
2. Choristers' Green, The Close
3. Fisherton Street
4. Tollgate Road
5. Salt Lane
6. The Close (from St John Street)

facing page:
Off Choristers' Green, The Close

The St John Street window, bottom right on this page, belongs to Malmesbury House, on the edge of the Cathedral Close. It is one of three forming the upper part of a two-storey bay, which like the Salt Lane window seen on page 85 is in the gothick style. Behind the window is a library of around 1760 with high quality plasterwork, which mixes medieval forms and classical details, in a way which later designers in the Gothic style would have thought quite improper. All the other windows on these pages derive from the classical tradition, though with widely differing degrees of orthodoxy.

1. Endless Street
2. Bedwin Street
3 & 4. Harnham Road
5. Castle Street

The three larger photos on this page all show what are generally known as 'venetian' windows, though 'palladian' is an occasional alternative. Why the form came to be connected with Venice is unclear, as is its relationship to the 16th century Italian architect Andrea Palladio. The Bedwin Street example, from Frowds Almshouses, is dated 1750, and its slightly ungainly glazing bar pattern would no doubt have been considered insufficiently refined 20 or 30 years later, when the Endless Street window was being put together. The one from Castle Street is likely to be late 19th or early 20th century in date.

salisbury **in detail**

1. Elm Grove Road
2. Shady Bower

salisbury **in detail**

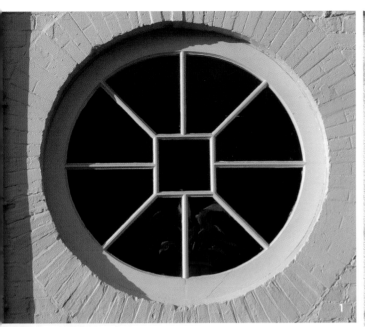

this page:
1. Rear of New Street
2. Malthouse Lane
3. Fisherton Street

facing page:
1. St Mark's Road
2. Bishop's Walk, The Close
3. Devizes Road

The Close window, top right on the facing page, is from a building probably dated 1661, which now houses the offices of the Cathedral's Chapter, its governing body. The brick arch above the window is known as a 'relieving arch', designed to prevent too much pressure being exerted on the flat head to the opening. It is a common structural device, though it is less common to see one being treated unashamedly as a design element, as it is here. Bottom left on this page is a window from the Playhouse. Part of an extension built in 2007, it is a good example of a simple, elegant modern design.

this page:
1. Lower Road
2. Choristers' Green, The Close
3. Harnham Mill

facing page:
Bridge Street

On the facing page is a window from the eastern part of the former County Hotel, dated 1874 and Italian Gothic in style. One of the city's most stately and impressive buildings, it is mainly of Ham Hill limestone, though the window's central shaft is a red sandstone, probably from the Midlands. On this page the Close window at top right dates from the early 14th century, no more than 100 years or so after the city's foundation. Below it is a later medieval opening from Harnham Mill, which was originally built as a paper mill, while the Lower Road window to the left is a typical example from the 17th century.

1

2

The left-hand window on this page is from the building on the north east corner of the market place, very successfully repaired and revealed in 2006. It is the one surviving original window, dating from the late 15th century. The use of clear glass in the repair work, rather than leaded lights, reflects the fact that the room behind was originally a workshop, rather than part of a house, and the opening was probably originally unglazed. The Crane Street window to its right is from Church House, and is typical of its early 17th century date, apart from an unusual design for the horizontal transom in the middle. Within the window there are several mismatches between the shapes of the vertical jambs and mullion (the central upright), and the transom and head which they join. The result is that the stonework looks unfinished, but this is such a common feature in Wiltshire stone buildings of the period that it was obviously deliberate, for reasons which are unclear. On the facing page, the right-hand window is from the North Canonry, on the west side of the Close. The prominently displayed initials 'RH' refer to nobody known to be connected with the house during the second half of the 17th century, when the window was added, and remain a mystery.

salisbury **in detail**

this page:
1. Crane Street
2. Rear of West Walk, The Close
3. Harnham Mill
4. West Walk, The Close

facing page:
1. Endless Street
2. Crane Street

this page:
1. Wilton Road
2. Milford Street
3. Catherine Street
4. West Walk, The Close

facing page:
Brown Street

The top window on this page is from the Salisbury Law Courts building, completed in 2009. Its carefully executed brickwork is a successful exercise in matching the city's Fisherton Grey bricks, which were manufactured only a few hundred yards away, with production ceasing some time early in the 20th century. The Law Courts bricks come from Holland. The two horizontal bands across the windows are known as transoms, like the equivalent feature in stone on page 96. Here they result from a need to maintain a degree of privacy in the room behind, generated by its function within the courts system.

09

a miscellany

Not all details from the city's buildings, or from the spaces between them, can be neatly sorted into categories, but many of the ones that can't still deserve to be shown, so this section is for them. There is by definition no common theme to bind them, so they are presented as individual objects, sometimes with stories to tell outside the mainstream of building design and construction. The story told by the sign on this page, which can be found on the edge of the coach park, is one of how much the world has changed, in probably no more than 70 or 80 years. Back then access to a telephone was worth flagging up, whereas now the equivalent sign, if there was any need for one, would point downwards, towards people's pockets. On the next page, the long-redundant lifting device in Guilder Lane tells us how the city has altered, the diversity of its long industrial past now just an occasional shadow amid modern streets of houses and shops and offices. Slightly further on is a structure of unclear purpose, by a railway line, possibly still with a vital role to play in the movement of trains, but more likely to have been left stranded by change, like the bollards and post on subsequent pages. Our surroundings are subtly enriched by these pointers to a different past, reminders of a world slightly but immeasurably distant.

09

salisbury **in detail**

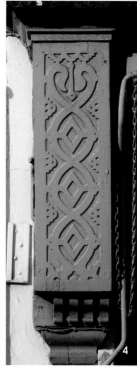

On this page the 'sunburst' plaque, bottom left, is an insurance company badge, used during the Georgian period, and into the Victorian. Each company had its own fire brigade, and news of a fire might bring several of these to the scene. Only a serious fire would persuade them to stay, however, if their own company's mark was not visible on the building. Above, the middle bracket has no actual function, but is one of three added to a 16th century house by Georgian refacers who felt that the projecting, or 'jettied', upper floor, which had managed unaided for 200 years, needed something to make it look properly secure.

this page:
1. Wilton Road
2. St Ann Street
3 & 4. Fisherton Street

5. Brown Street
6. Winchester Street

facing page:
1. Castle Street
2. St Nicholas Road
3. Milford Street
4. New Canal

5. Dews Road
6. Castle Street
7. Guilder Lane

this page:
1. New Canal
2. Ashley Road
3. Railway sidings

facing page:
1 & 4. Winchester Street
2, 3 & 5. Rollestone Street

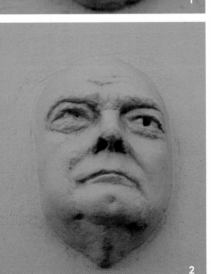

The five heads on this page come from the former Old George Inn, on the corner of Winchester Street and Rollestone Street, a building with a history typical of many in Salisbury. It has roof timbers dating back to about 1500, the facades were rebuilt in the mid 17th century, and the windows and doorway were remodelled around 1800. There are a total of eight heads, set into the tops of the ground floor windows. The fact that there are only five designs, three of them used twice, shows that the heads are cast not carved, and they are almost certainly the only known examples in Salisbury of Coade stone. This was an artificial material which enjoyed great popularity in the late 18th and early 19th centuries, being used for a variety of decorative objects as a substitute for natural stone. It was not a cement-based material, but a ceramic one, based on clay and fired in kilns. There is obviously some similarity to terracotta, but extra ingredients were added to Coade stone to increase its hardness. The material takes its name from Mrs Eleanor Coade, who successfully initiated and oversaw its manufacture from 1769 to 1821, a period when businesses run by women were very much the exception.

this page:
1 & 3. Milford Street
2. Lower Road
4. High Street

facing page:
St John Street

The carved wooden sheep on this page is not necessarily a ram, since it is likely to represent a Wiltshire Horn, a once common breed both genders of which have horns. It was put up when the shop below was used by Stonehenge Woollen Industries Ltd, a firm set up around 1900 in the Woodford Valley, with the aim of regenerating the rural economy. It had wider social motives than simply profit, typified by the employment of disabled servicemen after World War I. Local women were able to knit for the firm on a piecework basis, and it was successful enough to have three other shops in London. It ceased trading around 1960.

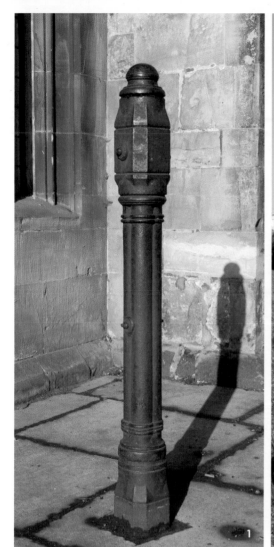

this page:
1. Crane Street
2. London Road
3. Tollgate Road

facing page:
1. Southampton Road
2. Laverstock Road
3. New Street

salisbury **in detail**

THE
NEW INN
at Salisbury

GARDEN
COURTYARD
WITH
CATHEDRAL
VIEWS

this page:
1. Harnham Gate, The Close
2. Central Car Park
3. Spire View

facing page:
1. Fisherton Street
2. Blackwell Mews

The landscaping above is in the middle of the Spire View housing, north of Fisherton Street. It is not here by chance - a tunnel carrying a channel linked to the river system runs underneath, making building here impossible. Salisbury was once surrounded by an extensive network of water meadows, through which water was diverted from its rivers to raise the temperature and enable grass to start growing earlier in the year, enhancing the grazing available for sheep. The remains of this system can be seen in many places, even as close to the city centre as these houses, and some of it is still operational.

1

2

10

chimneys

Traditionally, chimneys were necessities often turned to good advantage as opportunities for added decoration. Their prominence above the main bulk of a building created the potential for statements to be made, sometimes about a commitment to a particular design style, but more often a general message about a client's keenness to add value by doing more than just the bare minimum. Salisbury lacks any examples of this tendency which go quite as far as the bravura of some Tudor brick chimneys, but it still has cases which take the chimney some way beyond a mere device for getting rid of smoke. On this page the added value is achieved simply and economically, by using clay chimneypots made to a standard pattern. This particular chimney is from Endless Street. The following pages mix chimneys which go quite a lot further, such as the remarkably elegant and unusual late 19th century example from Wain-a-long Road, with ones where the effect is partly achieved by a happy accident, such as the family of chimney pots quietly not bothering anyone high up above Lower Road. Scanning the higher reaches of Salisbury's buildings from time to time can be quite rewarding.

10

this page:
1. Winchester Street
2. Salt Lane
3. Lower Road
4. Wilton Road

facing page:
Wain-a-long Road

1. Crane Street
2. Bridge Street
3. West Walk, The Close

1. Lower Road
2. Manor Road
3. Exeter Street
4. Bedwin Street

11

turrets, cupolas, finials & weathervanes

Features that protrude above the roofline for decorative purposes might be the definition of this section's contents. Chimneys also protrude, of course, but they have an initial function, even if they're often used to add decoration as well. A cupola is a small domed turret, usually rising from the central part of a roof, while finial is a general term for a decorative finish to a vertical feature. The two on this page are a good example of the Victorian use of terracotta to add value to a roofline, in this case with some fine detail which unfortunately can't be fully appreciated from the ground. The city's cupolas, as can be seen on the following pages, were often treated as highly important elements of a building's design, and finished with a level of skill and care that makes them worth more than just a passing glance. Some of the other features shown here are less sophisticated, and one or two verge on the eccentric, but they all play their part in making rooftop Salisbury a surprising and rewarding place.

11

The Poultry Cross finial and cross, on the facing page and this page respectively, follow the Gothic style of the original 15th century building, but like the rest of the upper parts they were added in 1853. The rather rounded and knobbly character, accentuated by weathering, is typical of later medieval patterns. Given a free rein, the mid-century Victorians tended to follow slightly earlier models. The timber and glass turret above, from the former Old Manor hospital, highlights the importance of maintenance. Just one missing piece of glass in this position can allow enough rainwater to penetrate to cause serious damage.

salisbury **in detail**

this page:
1. Brown Street
2. Poultry Cross

facing page:
1. Wilton Road
2. Poultry Cross

this page:
1. Love Lane
2. Wyndham Road
3. High Street
4. Church Lane, Lower Bemerton

facing page:
1. Devizes Road
2. Brewery Lane
3. Highbury Avenue

The cupola on the right on this page is from Matrons' College, in the Close. It is classical in design, dating from 1682. Sir Christopher Wren has traditionally been associated with the building, but more because of his friendship with the almshouse's founder, Bishop Seth Ward, than because of documentary or stylistic evidence. In fact it was probably designed by the builder, Thomas Glover of Harnham. The original building contract survives, and here the cupola is called a 'Cubulo', and required to be 'open quite down into the passage'. In other words, it lights the internal space below, meaning that it might also be called a lantern.

1. Fisherton Street
2. Mill Road
3. Castle Street
4. Behind Wilton Road
5. Off Choristers' Green, The Close

salisbury **in detail**

1. Wilton Road
2. Castle Street
3. Bedwin Street

The finials on this page, as on others in the section, derive from various design traditions or none. This high up, a designer might be subject to fewer constraints, and some fairly individual objects resulted. This is also the case with weathervanes, which, like sundials, have a notional function now displaced by the opportunities they provide for decorative flights of fancy. On the facing page, the cupola of 1906 from the post office is a more sober object, but still without any precise design precedent, and the architect, W.T. Oldrieve, seems to have indulged himself rather more here than on the rest of the building.

this page:
1. The Avenue
2. North Walk, The Close
3. Mill Road
4. St Martin's Church Street
5. Queen Street
6. Exeter Street

facing page:
Castle Street

turrets, cupolas, finials & weathervanes

12

carvings

The shaping of hard materials, particularly stone and wood, in order to construct and decorate buildings is a very old tradition, and one that played a fundamental part right at the start of Salisbury's story. The building of the cathedral, which started in 1220, involved the shaping of massive amounts of Chilmark and Purbeck stone, and of oak. Most of this was work that would not actually be termed 'carving'. If masons are shaping stones to form elements of buildings, even when the shapes are quite elaborate, they are 'working' them, with the term carving restricted to the addition of decoration. The results of that additional process, in

stone and timber, are shown in this section, including examples that predate 1220 and were originally at Old Sarum. A wide range is covered, from objects which were carefully designed beforehand to ones left entirely to the carver's imagination, and from grand sculptural set-pieces to small scale enrichments. All play their part in making the city a much more interesting place than it would have been if function alone had ruled supreme. The carving above, one of many from both outside and inside the Blue Boar Row Lloyds Bank building of 1869, is a good example.

12

this page:
1. Exeter Street
2 & 3. Southampton Road
4. Harnham Gate, The Close

facing page:
Blue Boar Row

The term 'gargoyle' comes from an old French word meaning 'throat', and strictly speaking refers to carvings which incorporate pipes, to throw rainwater clear of a building. In practice it tends to be used for any projecting carving which is based on humans or animals and interpreted with an element of humour or grotesqueness, as with the three heads on the facing page. The lower one is from the mid 14th century, while the upper ones are some 550 years later. Similar things are still being carved with great relish today. The grand group from the top of Lloyds Bank in Blue Boar Row is in an entirely different tradition, carefully designed and very serious. Unfortunately its exact significance is now unclear, and some of the fine detail is rather wasted at this height. The stone used is Portland, one of the most durable of British limestones, and well chosen for this lofty and exposed location. The coarser Ham Hill stone from Somerset, which is the principal one used in the building below, would not have been suitable for this sculpture.

this page:
1. New Canal
2. St Ann Street
3. Blue Boar Row
4. West Walk, The Close

facing page:
New Street

this page:
1. High Street Gate, The Close
2. Minster Street
3. Fisherton Street
4. St Nicholas Road
5. St John Street
6. Crane Street

facing page:
Ox Row

Centre top on the facing page, the idiosyncratic shapes from
New Sarum House in Minster Street are typical of its always lively
Salisbury-based architect, Fred Bath. Below, the Ionic capital
from the White Hart in St John Street is more orthodox. It dates
from around 1820, about 80 years before New Sarum House. To
the left, the statue of Edward VII on the High Street Gate was
put in place in 1902, taking over from a very decayed and
unidentifiable figure of a 17th century king. The carving on this
page, from Ox Row, is probably early 20th century in date, and
does not slavishly follow any conventional design tradition.

The two timber beasts, on this page and the facing one, are from a splendid building of 1878 on the corner of Winchester Street and Queen Street. The way the long one is formed with a projecting head, and then a body incorporated into the timber framing, is unusual and imaginative. The incised plasterwork above and below is a form of decoration known as pargetting. Top left on this page is carving from one of the two posts at the entrance to the Old George Mall. This one is a survival from the 14th century, unlike the other which is a modern imitation. The panel bottom right is from a house of around 1800, and may be of stone, but it could possibly have been cast in an artificial version of the material, such as Coade stone, examples of which can be seen on page 105. The layers of paint which now cover it make it impossible to say. To the left of this is some Portland stonework from a bank on the corner of Minster Street and the Cheesemarket. As befits the serious purpose of the building, this is designed to reproduce classical patterns as faithfully as possible. The details include such things as triglyphs, metopes, mutules and guttae, but happily it is perfectly possible to appreciate the building without having a clue what these words mean.

this page:
1. Queen Street
2. West Walk, The Close
3. Chipper Lane

facing page:
1. Old George Mall
2. Winchester Street
3. Minster Street
4. St Ann Street

carvings

this page:
1, 3 and 4. Exeter Street
2. Winchester Street

facing page:
Queen Street

The three stones from Exeter Street date from the 12th century, and come from the former cathedral at Old Sarum, which was abandoned once it had been decided to build a new one. They are now in the Close wall, which dates from the years after 1330, and contains many such examples of recycling. The two stone beasts are from the building at the corner of Winchester Street and Queen Street, and are further examples of its high-quality decoration. The one on this page shows the effects of air pollution, with a blackened skin forming which is beginning to cause decay. The parts washed by the rain remain clean and in good condition.

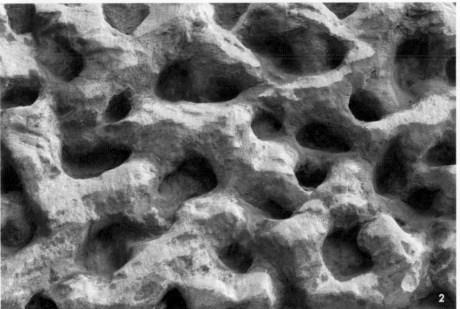

this page:
1. Bridge Street
2. Guildhall
3. Castle Street
4. Crane Street

facing page:
1. West Walk, The Close
2. Minster Street
3. High Street
4. Endless Street

salisbury **in detail**

MCMXXXV

The stonework top left on this page, from what is now Salisbury Museum, forms the roof to the porch, and is a type known as a fan vault. It dates from the 15th century, and is a very early example of the use in Salisbury of Ham Hill stone, from Somerset. The appearance of this type of stone here is no doubt linked to the building's function, prior to the Reformation, as the Salisbury residence of the Abbot of Sherborne, where the stone was well known. Later the building became known as the King's House, after James 1 stayed there in 1610 and 1613. Ham Hill stone did not reappear in the city until the 19th century, and its use in the

High Street example at bottom left is from well into the 20th. The other two features on this page, although in a similar colour range, are actually of Bath stone, which can lose its natural pale yellow tone and go rather brown in some conditions of polluted air. On the facing page, the pitted stonework from the Guildhall of 1788 is an example of vermiculation, a type of decoration carved into stones with the original intention of resembling the burrowings and delvings of earthworms.

The angel on the facing page is one of six from the Poultry Cross, 15th century in date and in Chilmark stone. The major volume on Salisbury's buildings produced by the Royal Commission on Historical Monuments, in 1980, stated that the angels' shields have 'traces of heraldic colouring, *barry of eight, or and azure*'. This is not a failure of proof reading but the language of heraldry, impenetrable to outsiders. Sadly, the only paint now visible is a piece of graffiti, which has added crude spectacles to one of the angels. The splendid carving on this page is one of two flanking a small doorway to an outhouse, hardly likely to have been its original position. It may have started life as a boss, that is to say a carved stone at the intersection of the ribs which form the basic structure of a vault. It is of Chilmark stone, so it must have originated locally, but beyond that its antecedents are a complete mystery. Although medieval in style, the date seems more likely to be 19th century.

this page: Rear of Endless Street
facing page: Poultry Cross

13

door heads & fanlights

Door heads are simply the upper parts of doorways, which have their own section in this book. There are times when it is worth focusing on the heads alone because the lower parts have been spoiled by the door being changed for something less in keeping, while in other cases the essence of the design is in the upper parts, and showing the whole dilutes the impact. A further reason for separating out the tops from the rest of doorways is the intervention of the realities of urban life, with the constant presence of parked cars frequently preventing a complete photograph. In the case of the Endless Street door head on this page, cars were the initial

reason for not using an image of the whole doorway, but in fact focusing on the upper part alone has its own reward. Here we have, in a quiet side street, a vivid replica of stylistic elements perfected on the shores of the Mediterranean two thousand years ago, transplanted into a substantial but not palatial English house, from the late eighteenth century. The whole building is of high quality, but it has little out and out ornamentation beyond this dazzling miniature temple front above the front door, proudly welcoming visitors.

13

salisbury **in detail**

On the facing page is a display of fanlights, one of the most characteristic and attractive facets of Georgian houses. While the name indicates the semi-circular shape found in many examples, the word's meaning has been extended to cover any small window immediately above a door, and within an overall surround. The door head on this page is a 'shell hood', an 18th century design which aims at an effect slightly beyond the commonplace. This one is actually from the late 19th century, when a general Victorian dislike of Georgian architecture was fading away, and revival of the style became acceptable.

facing page:
1. Bedwin Street
2. Chipper Lane
3. Endless Street
4. New Street

this page:
Churchfields Road

this page:
St Ann Street

facing page:
1. Crane Street
2. Estcourt Road
3. Hulse Road

The door head on this page actually predates the late 18th century house of which it is now part by some 50 years, showing that a desire to be up-to-date, seen in many Georgian refacings of older buildings, did not necessarily outweigh appreciation of earlier designs. The two late 19th century pale-coloured terracotta examples on the facing page are both identical, illustrating how the material lent itself to repeat production. What is unique here is the fact that one of them is partly buried, by a wall not obviously later in date, a curiosity which would seem to indicate some confusion during the building process, to say the least.

salisbury **in detail**

this page:
1. Crane Street
2. Chipper Lane
3. Bridge Street
4. New Street

facing page:
Choristers' Green, The Close

On this page the door heads range in time from the 15th century, the date of the earliest parts of Church House in Crane Street, to 1906, when the post office in Chipper Lane was built. The example from the former County Hotel in Bridge Street, with its date of 1893, is a conscious throwback to themes of almost 600 years earlier, echoing as it does the early 14th century tombs of two bishops, Roger de Mortival and Simon of Ghent, in the cathedral choir. The coat of arms on the facing page is that of Charles Mompesson and his wife Elizabeth, and is located above the front door to the house in the Close which bears his family's name.

All the door heads on these two pages have stylistic themes derived in some sense from the classical tradition, but none of them has any ambition to recreate the essence of a Greek or Roman temple in a street in Salisbury, in the way that the head on the first page of the section does. The pair on the facing page from Swaynes Close, in particular, is a remarkably individualistic creation, using identifiably classical motifs in brick and stone to produce an overall effect that has no obvious parallels anywhere, while the Elm Grove Road example on this page is a minor tour de force in an otherwise quite restrained house.

this page:
1. Elm Grove Road
2. Blue Boar Row
3. Wilton Road
4. Park Lane

facing page:
1. Hamilton Road
2. Swaynes Close

salisbury **in detail**

14

window heads

Window heads merit their own section for similar reasons to door heads - it enables attention to be focused on what is sometimes the most design-rich part of a window surround, without being distracted by any unfortunate alterations to the functional part of the window. The splendid example on this page, from Lloyds Bank in Castle Street, has the bold and heavy forms best characterised as baroque, though its date of 1901 marks it down as belonging to a revival of that style. To have participated in its original flowering, the building would have needed to have been a couple of centuries or so earlier. The years around 1900 were a fruitful period

for architecture in Salisbury, and the window head on the final page of the section is another good example from those times. It comes from one of the finest houses in the city, Hillcote in Manor Road, which was built in 1896, and which contributes details to four other sections of the book as well.

14

this page:
1. Castle Street
2 & 3. Shady Bower
4. Catherine Street
5. St Ann Street

facing page:
Manor Road

15

terracotta

Terracotta (Italian for 'baked earth') is a material closely related to brick, though generally using a finer form of clay. After a brief period of popularity in the 16th century, it came into its own again in the second half of the 19th, when it was widely used in many types of buildings, including grand ones such as the Albert Hall. In Salisbury it is mainly found in the form of ornament for domestic buildings, though the example above comes from a building in Salt Lane which actually started out as a fire station. This was first built in 1906, and doubled in size a few years later, when the terracotta decoration was carefully repeated. Even functional municipal buildings were felt to merit such ornamental additions. The material is often brick-red in colour, as above, though buff-coloured examples are also fairly common. A variant is known as faience (again Italian in origin, from the town of Faenza), which is a glazed form of terracotta, developed towards the end of the 19th century. It was valued for its added ease of cleaning, though in Salisbury its use seems to have been restricted mainly to shopfronts. Together, the various forms of terracotta make a major contribution to the visual appeal of Victorian and Edwardian buildings in the city.

15

The finest terracotta in Salisbury is to be found on a building in Fisherton Street, originally built in the 1860s as 'Swift's Temperance [i.e. alcohol-free] Hotel'. The photos on the left and top right of this page show examples from it. The ground floor has been lost to shop fronts, but happily the decoration to the floors above survives. An additional stroke of fortune means that, for once, we can tell where the terracotta was made. The rectangular panel bears, in its bottom left hand corner, the stamp 'DOULTON LAMBETH', indicating a London origin. Most of the other large-scale manufacturers were based in the Midlands, and there is no

evidence of any local production of terracotta. This building was clearly known to Thomas Hardy, since in Jude the Obscure he has Jude stopping for a meal at a temperance hotel 'in the street leading from the station' after arriving at Melchester (the name Hardy used for Salisbury in his novels). He then crosses the 'town bridge' and 'turns the corner into the Close'. Not surprisingly, Hardy was copying the geography of Salisbury fairly exactly, rather than going to the bother of making things up.

this page:
1. Bourne Avenue
2. Fowlers Road
3. Estcourt Road
4. Bourne Avenue
5. Pennyfarthing Street

facing page:
1 & 2. Fisherton Street
3. Salt Lane

this page:
1. Fisherton Street
2. Manor Road
3 & 4. Bourne Avenue
5. Milford Hill
6. Fisherton Street

facing page:
Fisherton Street

The three heads on these pages emphasise the remarkable quality of the temperance hotel decoration, while the Milford Hill example makes good use of the colour contrast with vitrified bricks. This motif occurs on several houses, both in Milford Hill and in Rampart Road nearby. Architectural terracotta was generally produced using plaster moulds, lending itself to repeat production, though the moulds wore out and could not be used indefinitely. In many other cases, such as the temperance hotel roundels, pieces of decoration shown in this book occur only once in Salisbury, though they may have been used again elsewhere.

terracotta

this page:
1. Exeter Street
2. Manor Road
3. Love Lane
4. New Street
5. Manor Road

facing page:
Castle Sreet

salisbury **in detail**

The decoration on the top of the facing page includes sunflowers, and several other pieces of terracotta in this section should probably also be interpreted as representing them. The sunflower was adopted as an emblem of the Aesthetic Movement, which flourished in the late 19th century, with Oscar Wilde its most prominent figure in England. The movement emphasised art as something to be valued for its own sake, rather than for any moral or utilitarian reasons, and its devotees used the sunflower to declare their adherence to the cause. The symbolism is now ineffective, but luckily the decorative value lives on.

this page:
1. Moberley Road
2 & 3. Manor Road

facing page:
1. Fowlers Road
2. Kelsey Road
3. Wilton Road

this page:
1. Belle Vue Road
2. Bourne Avenue
3 & 4. Manor Road
5 & 6. Ox Row

facing page:
Southampton Road

Faience is fairly uncommon in Salisbury, but when found is generally of superb quality, as in the examples bottom right on this page, from an Ox Row shop front. Art nouveau lettering is also part of the shop design, indicating an early 20th century date. Three of the terracotta examples on this page use 'egg and dart' ornament, which is a motif from the architecture of ancient Greece and Rome. Where decorative sources can be identified they tend to be classical, rather than from the alternative Gothic style, which was beginning to run out of steam by the time of domestic terracotta's late Victorian heyday.

16

plaques and coats of arms

Plaques can be generally defined as decorative tablets in stone or metal, and less frequently other materials, attached to buildings with the intention of conveying information. This will usually be in the form of lettering, but some form of symbols may also be used. The example on this page comes under the latter heading, and illustrates how a lot can be said without the use of any words at all. Carved onto the plaque are gyves, an old word meaning fetters or shackles, and the stone is an eloquent remnant of what was once Salisbury's principle gaol, on the south side of Fisherton Street just west of the Avon. All that remains of the building is a

stretch of walling with two barred windows set into it, surviving only because it was used in the plinth on which the clocktower of 1890 was built. One of the windows can be seen on page 75 and the clocktower on page 179. There is inevitably an overlap between this section and the one on lettering, and several more plaques can be found there.

16

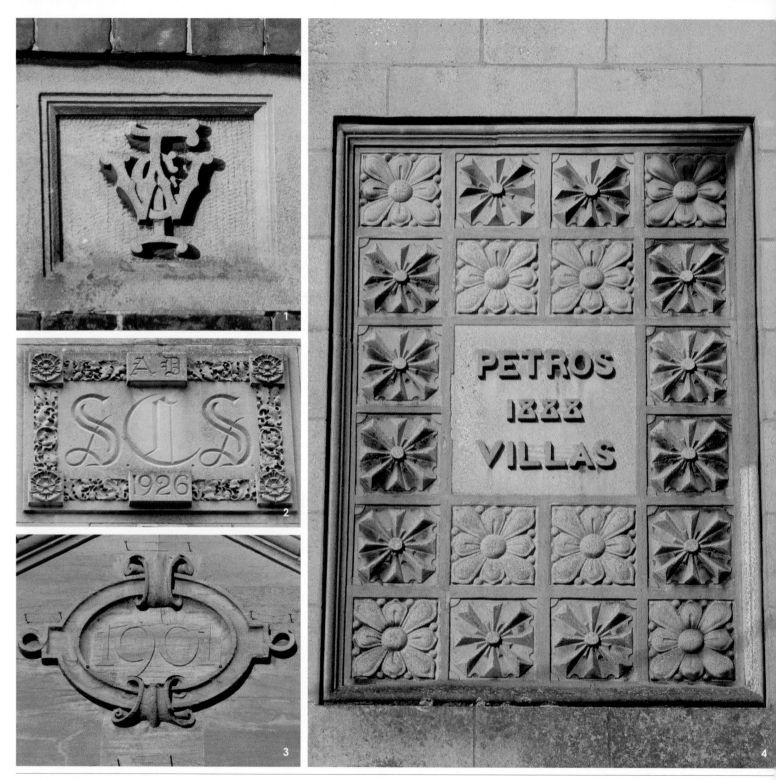

Endowed by
Thomas Taylor
Alderman of this City
1698

On this page is a plaque from Taylors Almshouses in Bedwin Street, recording their original construction in 1698, rather than their rebuilding in 1886. On the facing page, the SCS of 1926 records the former premises of the Salisbury Co-operative Society. A sprung dance floor is believed to survive in the room behind, long unused. Petros Villas is of interest because it is one of several buildings on the Devizes Road which are early examples of concrete construction. The plaque itself is not of stone, as it would have been in earlier periods, but of cement.

this page:
Bedwin Street

facing page:
1. Wilton Road
2. Winchester Street
3. Castle Street
4. Devizes Road

this page:
1. Crane Street
2. Bedwin Street
3. High Street Gate, The Close
4. St Ann Place
5. Winchester Street
6. Castle Street

facing page:
Off Choristers' Green, The Close

Top left on this page is a symbolic plaque, denoting ownership by the Freemasons of their Hall in Crane Street. The Municipal Charities, whose plaque below is another from Taylors Almshouses in Bedwin Street, no longer exist under that name, but have been absorbed into a modern body, the Salisbury City Almshouse and Welfare Charities. Both this Taylors plaque and the one on the page before have used a hard and fine-grained Purbeck stone for the lettering, rather than the coarser Ham Hill stone of the surrounds.

There are differing styles of royal coats of arms on this page and the facing one, both probably dating from the reign of Charles II. In a subsidiary position at Matrons' College, on this page, is a more modest episcopal coat of arms, that of Bishop Seth Ward, who founded the almshouse in 1682. The surviving building contract, already referred to on page 124, is of great interest for the detail into which it goes in specifying how the almshouse should be put together. Rather surprising to modern eyes is the stipulation that 'mortar shall be made of 1 quarter of lime to each load of earth'. The exact meaning of this clause is open to interpretation, but it is hard to escape the conclusion that 'earth' meant much the same then as it does now, and that in an area lacking very abundant sources of easily accessible local sand, somewhat less pure aggregates were being pressed into service. A loamy mix would also improve the workability of the mortar, though not necessarily its long term durability. Whatever the exact composition of the mixture the bricklayers were working with, it is unlikely to have conformed to any recent British Standards.

plaques and coats of arms

17

sundials & clockfaces

There are more clocks around than sundials, but the latter tend to be more photogenic. This is hardly surprising, since for quite a while now no-one has put a sundial up because they had any serious desire to tell the time from it. This leaves them as decorative objects, and the resulting opportunities have been responded to with a rich variety of designs, a few of which can be seen on these pages. The one above was added to the front wall of a house on Paynes Hill around 1980, and combines a simple design with some Latin, which translates as 'The footsteps of man were always gentle upon the earth'. Both Latin and English contribute to the large number of mottoes, generally more obviously relevant, which appear on sundials, often exploiting the potential for cheerfulness - 'I count only the sunny hours' - but occasionally on the gloomy side, making a comparison between the passing sun and the transience of human life. The sundials on public view in Salisbury have messages based on both these approaches. Clocks are of course rather more practical mechanisms, but still provide opportunities for decoration. This is probably just as well, since some of the older ones visible from the city's streets do not always inspire confidence in their complete accuracy as timekeepers.

17

LIFE'S BUT A WALKING SHADOW

IA 49

VI
V
IIII
III
II

VII
VIII
IX
X
XI
XII
I

22 DEC
4 FEB
9 FEB
6 MAR
21 MAR
6 APRIL
21 APRIL
6 MAY
22 MAY
22 JUNE

24 AUGUST
8 AUGUST
23 JULY
22 JUNE

THIS IS LIFE ETERNAL THAT
THEY MAY KNOW THEE THE ONLY
TRUE GOD. AND JESUS CHRIST.
WHOM THOU HAST SENT.
ST JOHN. CHAPTER 17. VERSE 3.

The dial from Malmesbury House, on the facing page, is a constant attraction for visitors to the Close, while the one on this page is from Trinity Hospital. Its sunburst decoration was produced in the cathedral workshops in the 1970s, and is lead which has been gilded, meaning that it is covered with a layer of gold about 0.0001mm in thickness. The cheerful face in the centre was cast from one carved in stone. The Fisherton Street clocktower of 1890 is described by Nikolaus Pevsner, in his 'Buildings of England' volume on Wiltshire, as 'a depressing Gothic erection in a position without distinction', which seems a bit harsh.

this page:
1. Fisherton Street
2. Trinity Street

facing page:
North Walk, The Close

this page:
1. St Thomas's Square
2. High Street
3. Dews Road
4. Mill Road

facing page:
New Canal

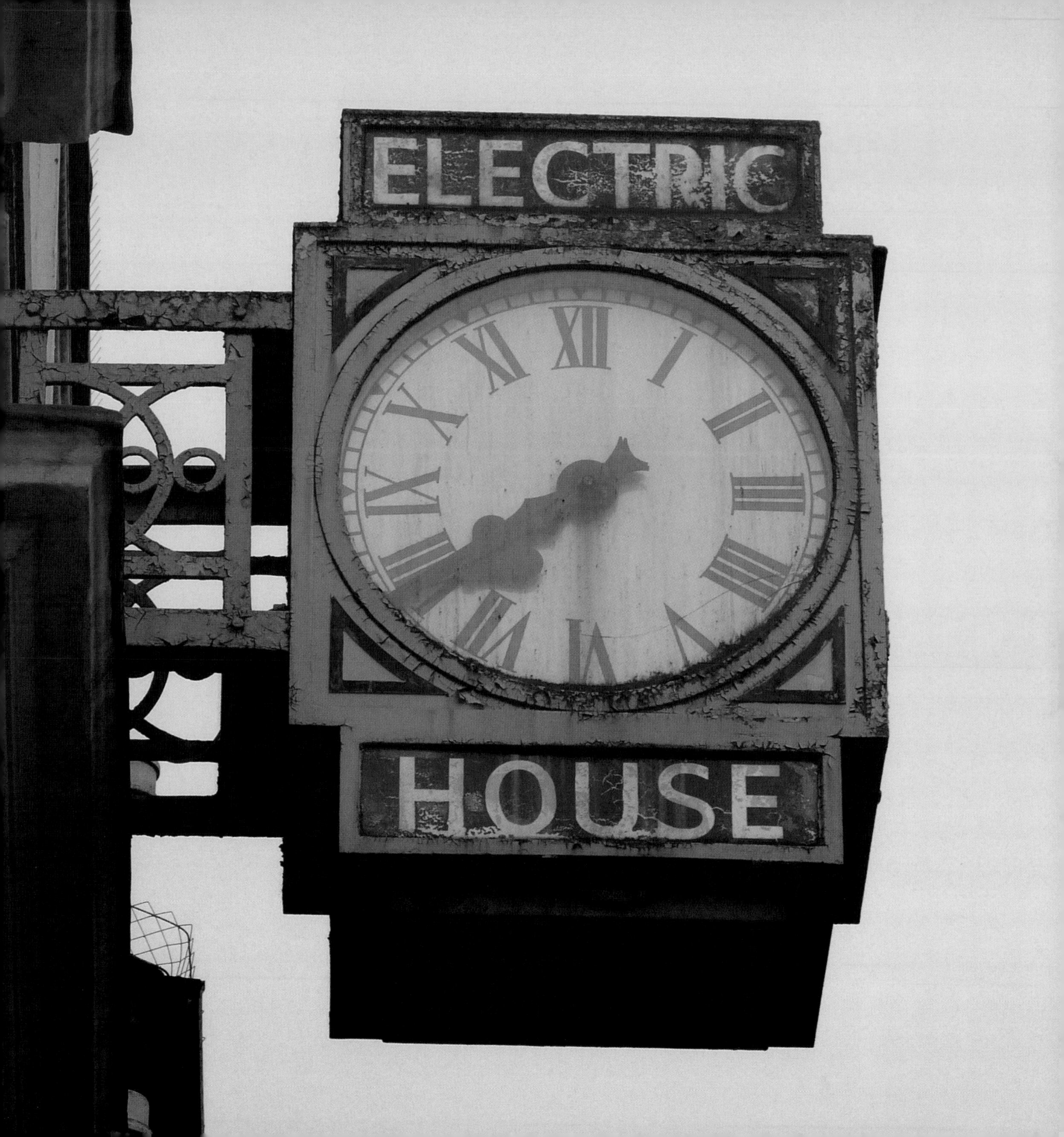
ELECTRIC
HOUSE

18

ironwork

Iron is a material whose use in connection with buildings goes back many centuries, valued both for its structural properties and the decoration that could be added to it. There are medieval tomb enclosures of ironwork inside the cathedral, but domestically most examples in Salisbury date from after 1700. The material's main subdivision is between wrought iron and cast iron, with significant differences between the two in terms of methods of converting from ore, and chemical structure. From the point of view of finished objects, however, the key distinction is that the former was generally shaped by hand ('wrought' is an archaic past tense of the verb 'to work'), and the latter cast in a mould. Repetitive patterns will tend to indicate manufacture by casting, as with this splendid veranda screen from the Southampton Road, probably late 19th century in date. Most if not all of this will have been cast in sections, forming a kit of parts which was then bolted or slotted together. Welding as a technique does not predate the 20th century, and in any case the later application of heat to cast elements is better avoided.

18

salisbury **in detail**

On this page the blue window cill metalwork from New Street is a particularly good example of what blacksmiths are capable of. This feature may well have taken a week or so to create. The 1902 boundary marker is cast iron, which of course has the great advantage of lending itself to repetitive production. There are at least four of these plates, in a line just beyond the station's northern platform, where they define a former division between the territories of two different railway companies. On the facing page the gate and its posts will have been made up with a combination of cast and wrought sections.

this page:
1. Fowlers Road
2. De Vaux Place
3. Railway Station
4. New Street

facing page:
1. Southampton Road
2. Fisherton Street
3. Blue Boar Row
4. Market Place
5. Scots Lane
6. Brown Street

The School Lane hinge is wrought iron, which has to be worked hot. Something similar created today would probably be done in mild steel, which to some extent can be shaped while cold. The cast iron circular feature was a ventilation grille, with the disc designed to move on a central pin. In Queen Street the gate, a mixture of cast and wrought iron, has been fixed open and is clearly redundant, but happily has been left in place. The non-painted metalwork at the station is steel, now more commonly used than either type of iron. It is stronger and cheaper to produce, but less likely to have decoration added to it.

this page:
1. St Ann Place
2. School Lane
3. Queen Street

facing page:
Railway Station

Both gate and railings are cases where wrought and cast iron have been incorporated in the same feature. The decorative parts of the railings will have been cast, but the shape of the uprights is a good clue that these were wrought. Had they been cast, they would have broken under whatever impact has been at work here, rather than gently bending. The brittleness of cast iron is one of its key features. Rust, which is now clearly visible in the right-hand photo, is the chief enemy of ironwork, but the vagaries of humanity also take their toll. The Bedwin Street frontage of St Edmund's churchyard, with its low stone wall bearing only the cut-off stumps of railings, is a melancholy example of the melting down of ironwork during World War II. While the motive was understandable, the actual contribution to the war effort appears to have been minimal.

salisbury **in detail**

facing page:
1. Choristers' Green, The Close
2. North Walk, The Close

this page:
Fowlers Hill

This plate, forming the end of a tie to support a sagging structure, is the kind of feature to which cast iron was ideally suited. It would have been formed by pouring molten metal into a sand mould shaped by a wooden pattern, though plastic patterns are now sometimes used instead. The letters could easily be added to the mould, and if necessary varied to suit different customers. 'W. Rowland' may have been a small-scale local engineering firm, but it could also have been the name of an ironmonger.

19

lettering

Lettering is clearly not fundamental to buildings; it is an add-on, a feature aimed principally at the provision of information, but with plenty of potential for decorative value as well. It can take numerous forms, though the example on this page belongs to one of the less common ones, since the information element has got lost somewhere along the way. Best seen from platform 6 of the railway station, it can be unpicked to reveal an intention to advertise a business, almost certainly called Johnsons, which traded as drapers and milliners at 144 Fisherton Street, 'next to subway'. What other information is contained within the lettering is less clear, and what is entirely unclear is how two different goes at sign-writing, presumably of different periods, became mixed up together, resulting in a net information value of zero. This type of lettering, painted onto walls, tends to be temporary in nature, and this example is a fortunate survival, on a wall a few feet from the railway platform, with the space in between now an abandoned alleyway. The wall forms the side to premises which are certainly now numbered 144 Fisherton Street, and presumably were when the signs were painted, but how the 'subway' fits into the scenario is not clear.

19

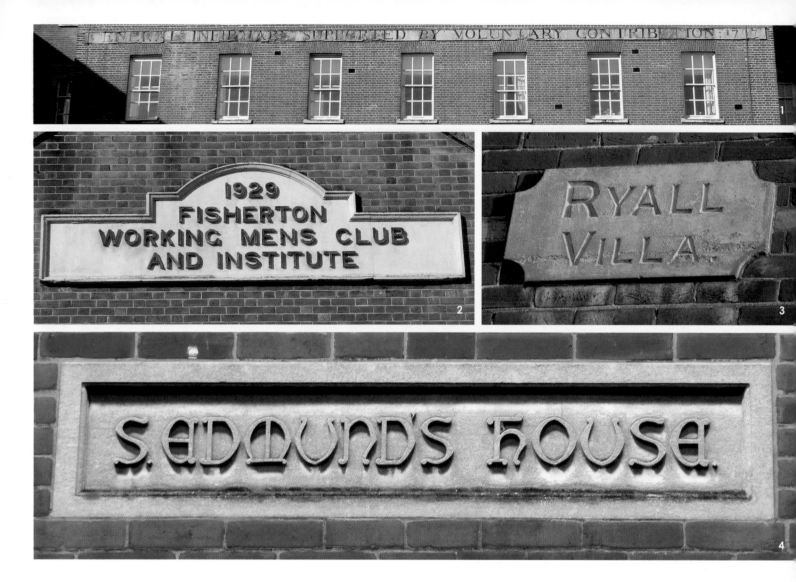

These pages show a wide range of styles and dates of lettering, some restricted to the barest minimum of necessary information, and some rather more discursive. At the top of this page the inscription on the former Salisbury Infirmary gives an indication of how the building was funded, as well as the date of 1767, and is notable because it is the only form of decoration on what is otherwise a very plain facade. There is certainly no clue that the designer was the notable Bath architect, John Wood the younger. The most informative of the pieces of lettering on the facing page records the two major dates in the history of Harnham Bridge.

The replacement of an 'e' with an apostrophe in 'widen'd' is probably in line with the style of the day, rather than being due to the letter cutter running out of space. In inscriptions of 150 years earlier it is not unknown for words to reach the edge of the plaque before completion, with the artist cheerfully cramming the leftover letters at a reduced size into the space above.

TEA & COFFEE

WAREHOUSE ESTD. 1776

E M A TERRACE.

43

Built in 1245 by BISHOP BINGHAM Widend in 1774

MENS WEAR

HAIR STUDIO

MOOSE HALL

facing page:
1. Fisherton Street
2 & 3. Wilton Road
4. Bedwin Street

this page:
1. New Canal
2. Catherine Street
3. Devizes Road
4. St Nicholas Road
5. Lower Road
6. Catherine Street

lettering

this page: Fisherton Street

facing page:
1. New Street
2. Ox Row
3. New Canal
4. St John Street

47 Fisherton Street has what was once among the finest shopfronts in the city, sadly defaced when all the projecting parts of its green faience (i.e. glazed terracotta) decoration were knocked off to enable it to be boarded up. Its quality is still evident, particularly in the art nouveau style of its lettering. Putting the shopfront back into its original condition would be possible, but it would not be cheap.

The Ox Row shopfront, centre left on this page, is another example of faience, again with an art nouveau feel. New Street and New Canal show Gothic-style lettering, of 1871 and 1881 respectively. The 'Literary and Scientific Institution' at one time housed Salisbury Art College. The simpler lettering in St John Street indicates the former premises of the stonemasonry business run by the Osmond family. There were two Osmonds, father and son but both called William, and from around 1820 into the 1880s the firm was closely involved with the cathedral. In the 1830s William senior became a friend of the leading early Victorian architect A.W.N. Pugin,

designer of St Osmund's church a couple of hundred yards away in Exeter Street, and was apparently persuaded by him of the virtues of the Gothic style. The St John Street building is firmly classical in style, which may suggest that it dates from before the Pugin connection.

1

28

2

CAMDEN TERRACE

3

OSBORNE TERRACE.

4

this page:
1. Fairview Road
2. Milford Street
3. Milford Hill
4. Windsor Road

facing page:
Fisherton Street

salisbury **in detail**

salisbury **in detail**

198

facing page:
1. Rear of New Canal
2. Nelson Road
3. Salt Lane
4. Off College Street
5. Wilton Road
6. Milford Hill

this page:
1. Endless Street
2. Railway Station
3. Rosemary Lane, The Close

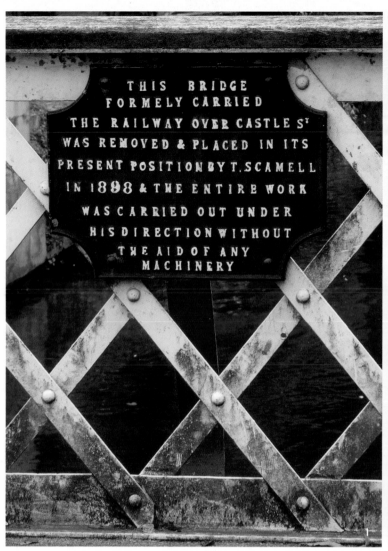

The plaque and manufacturers' lettering from Scamell's Bridge in Nelson Road tell its unusual story, along the way omitting an 'r' from the third word of the plaque. Another plate across the bridge is identical, except that the 'r' is back in place. Opposite, the art nouveau lettering in Bath stone is from the Young Gallery in Chipper Lane, already seen in the windows section. The street name plate on the previous page raises something of a philosophical question - if a street is truly Endless, can it actually lead to anywhere else? The name probably derives from the street having originally continued further north, beyond the city.

this page:
1. Nelson Road
2. Water Lane
3. Nelson Road

facing page:
Chipper Lane

salisbury **in detail**

R· GOGHGHER

ors BY the

PRICES OF

SALISBURY·

IOR· AND M

oriel windows

Oriel probably comes from a Latin word for 'gallery' or 'porch', and in the Middle Ages had a somewhat wider meaning than it does now. Subsequently it was narrowed down to mean specifically a window that projects from a building, and is not supported from the ground. An oriel is therefore a design feature that is structurally more complicated than an ordinary window, which can be formed by simply leaving an opening in a wall, but there were major compensations for the extra work involved. Expanded into three dimensions, this is a form of window that gives a designer free rein, either to develop themes already present in the overall design, or to add a different accent to the building. Salisbury has examples from almost all periods since its foundation, from the Middle Ages to the present, but the 18th and early 19th centuries were the oriel's heyday. Some were included as part of the design of new buildings, as with the oriel of around 1800 on this page, but the majority were additions to older buildings, often made when frontages were being changed to bring them more into line with current fashions. Oriel windows were an effective way of adding value to an elevation, and collectively they make a vital contribution to the city's character.

20

this page:
1. High Street
2. Castle Street

facing page:
1. Crane Street
2. Exeter Street
3. Queen Street
4. Milford Street

The 14th century stone example, top right on the facing page, is attached to the Close wall, near St Ann's Gate. It might be termed a turret rather than an oriel window, but the functional outcome is the same - a useful expansion of the room behind it, and views through 180 degrees. In fact this may have been the original motive for construction, the suggestion being that it was built for a watchman. The timber windows are however much later. On this page, what looks like stonework in the double decker oriel from Castle Street is actually cement, consistent with a date towards the end of the 19th century.

salisbury **in detail**

oriel windows

salisbury **in detail**

this page:
1. St Ann Street
2. St Nicholas Road

facing page:
1. St Edmund's Church Street
2. High Street
3. St John Street
4. Love Lane

oriel windows

The oriel on the facing page is from the southern end of the High Street, by the gateway into the Close, and is typical of the later 18th century. The building to which it belongs is almost certainly one advertised as a 'neat dwelling house' in the Salisbury Journal in 1788, probably not long after its construction. The angled three sided form of the oriel is one found all over the historic parts of the city, though the embellishment applied to the top and bottom is less common. The two oriels on this page are much more individual designs, with no direct parallels elsewhere in Salisbury.

this page:
1. Bridge Street
2. Minster Street

facing page:
High Street

oriel windows

The two oriels from Minster Street, on the bottom of this page, span a considerable period. The one on the left is one of the earliest timber oriels in the city, probably 15th century in date, while the other was constructed around 1900. It is part of New Sarum House, a building by Fred Bath with a remarkable array of details. Across the road from it is the building on the left of the facing page, very similar in date, and also exhibiting the self-confidence and verve typical of this period. Bottom right on the facing page, the Castle Road oriel is from an Arts and Crafts house of around 1930, already seen in the windows section.

1. Fish Row
2. Castle Street
3 & 4. Minster Street

1. Minster Street
2. Fish Row
3. Castle Road

this page:
1. New Canal
2. St Nicholas Road
3. Butcher Row
4. St Edmund's Church Street

facing page:
West Walk, The Close

The window in St Edmund's Church Street is of course not an oriel at all, but there is still a valid reason for having the photo here. The clue is in the brickwork immediately around the window, which looks different from that further out. Something has obviously happened here, and the likeliest explanation is that there was once an oriel and it has now gone, perhaps after a fire. The brickwork is in the centre of a short terrace of around 1800, just the sort of place where such a feature would have been found. Early photos of Salisbury show many oriels which have now disappeared, but happily a great number still survive.

This journey through Salisbury's streets will have revealed much about its buildings - not just their extraordinary quality, but also the contribution made by the humbler ones tucked away in quiet corners, the range of components and materials incorporated across the centuries, and the relatively few additions made to this stock of details by recent generations. The challenge now is to safeguard this remarkable legacy, without seeking to do so by preserving the city in aspic. Salisbury will continue to change, but it needs to do so while respecting the wealth of good things from its past, seeking new buildings that match the quality of earlier ones, without any obligation to copy their styles, and being aware of what it is that makes it a special place. If this book can add to that awareness, it will have more than justified its production.

For those who may wish to seek out some of the features glimpsed in the book's pages on the ground, maps with suggested routes for doing this are available on the Civic Society website:

www.salisburycivicsociety.org.uk